High Sierra
Hiking Guide #2

MOUNT ABBOT

**Mono Creek and Recesses, Bear Creek,
Silver Divide and vicinity**

by the editors of
WILDERNESS PRESS
Thomas Winnett
editor in chief
designed and illustrated by
Don Denison

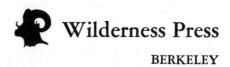 Wilderness Press

BERKELEY

Acknowledgments

We are very grateful for the hours of consultation we have enjoyed with fellow mountain-addicts, whose long and intense experiences in the Sierra have made their advice so valuable: Malcolm Burnstein, Phillip Burton, Sue Denison, Thomas Dum, Don Evers, Colin Fletcher, Don Harkin, Cecelia Hurwich, Rudolph Hurwich, John Jencks, Dick Kelty, Mary King, Richard Leonard, George Marks, John McElheney, Hugh Nash, David Pesonen, Phil Pister, David Poast, Chet Rice, Edwin Rockwell, Sue Schwenke, Genny Schumacher Smith, Helen Sharsmith, Bob and Evie Shephard, Daniel Simon, Bob Swanson, Jim Watters, Richard Wiebe, Caroline Winnett, Jason Winnett, Lu Winnett.

—the editors of Wilderness Press

PHOTO CREDITS

page ii	*Rose Lake*. U.S. Forest Service	
viii	U.S. Forest Service	
x	Karl Schwenke	
16	*Golden marmot*. National Park Service	
24	Thomas Winnett	
30	*Silver Divide*. U.S. Forest Service	

Introduction

The HIGH SIERRA HIKING GUIDES by the editors of Wilderness Press are the first *complete* guides to the famous High Sierra. Each guide covers one 15-minute U.S.G.S. topographic quadrangle, which is an area about 13 miles east-west by 17 miles north-south. The inside front cover shows the location of the quadrangle covered by this guide.

There is a great and increasing demand for literature about America's favorite wilderness, John Muir's "Range of Light." To meet this demand, we have undertaken this guide series. The purpose of each book in the series is threefold: first, to provide a reliable basis for planning a trip; second, to serve as a field guide while you are on the trail; and third, to stimulate you to further field investigation and background reading. In each guide, there are a minimum of 100 described miles of trails, and the descriptions are supplemented with maps, profiles and other logistical and background information. HIGH SIERRA HIKING GUIDES are based on first-hand observation. There is absolutely no substitute for walking the trails, so we walked all the trails.

In planning this series, we chose the 15-minute quadrangle as the unit because—though every way of dividing the Sierra is arbitrary—the quadrangle map is the chosen aid of almost every wilderness traveler. Inside the back cover of this book is a map of the quadrangle, showing described trails and good campsites. With this map, you can always get where you want to go, with a minimum of detours or wasted effort.

One other thing the wilderness traveler—the day hiker as well as the backpacker—will need: a permit from the Forest Service. You may obtain a permit at a Forest Service ranger station or office by indicating where you are going and when you will be there. The permits are also available by mail. If you don't know the address of the nearest Forest Service station or office, write the Regional Forester, 630 Sansome St., San Francisco, Calif. 94111.

Table of Contents

The Country

MT. ABBOT QUAD IS exciting mountaineer country. Rugged alpine heights dominate nearly one half of the map's area; the rest is taken up by forested watershed basins and valleys. The climactic Sierra crest backbones the east side of the map, and it is perpendicularly ribbed to the west by 4 divides. From north to south, these divides are the Silver Divide, the Mono Divide, the Mt. Hooper/Mt. Senger complex, and the Le Conte Divide (just off the southern edge of the map). These east-west ranges separate the drainages of Fish Creek, Mono Creek, Bear Creek, and the South Fork of the San Joaquin. All these drainages are tributaries of the great San Joaquin River,

> "I want free life, and I want fresh air . . .
> The green beneath and the blue above
> And dash, and danger, and life and love."
> F. Desprey, *Lasca*

and 2 reservoirs, Lake Thomas A. Edison and Florence Lake, interrupt the flows of Mono Creek and the South Fork of the San Joaquin River. Drainages east of the crest, though not shown in their entirety on this map, include McGee Creek, Hilton Creek and Rock Creek.

Fascination with this harsh and imposing terrain has many aspects. One is the sheer magnificence of the towering peaks, 8 of which exceed 13,000 feet in elevation. Reminders of the country's glacial saga remain behind in the form of 4 small glaciers, and Volcanic Knob is a black visual recollection of the fire and lava that once bubbled to the surface. Another aspect is the striking range of colors. The greens of the forest carpet border the severe grays and whites of the granites of the Sierra batholith, and the metamorphosed red and black rocks of the peaks at the east end of the Silver Divide compose an artist's pallet to contrast with the emerald greens of alpine lakes and the azure of Sierran skies.

This is a land of contrasts, where densely forested valley flats like those at old Kip Camp give way suddenly to barren cirque basins like those in the upper reaches of Hilgard Creek. First-time visitors are often alienated by the seemingly sterile alpine climes, and it is only after they come to realize the surprising wealth of life that exists in these ecological niches, and begin to know the fragile nature of the balance, that they warm to this land of rock and snow. The incredible beauty of these open rocky heights is compounded by the pregnant si-

> "We are thus living in the period of big cities. Deliberately the world has been amputated of all that constitutes its permanence: nature, the sea, hilltops, evening meditation."
>
> Camus, *Myth of Sisyphus*

lence that accompanies them—a silence broken only by

the splash and murmur of streams connecting strings of Paternoster lakes*. Since man first trod these granite lands, it has always been the magnificence of the scale, the pulsing silence and the sense of unaltered antiquity that have awed him, and this awe has convinced him that he should leave memorable places like this as he found them.

As a consequence, this region is protected by a Wilderness Area designation, which reserves it for public recreational use and prohibits commercial exploitation, road encroachment and travel by mechanized conveyance. Appropriately enough, this Wilderness Area is named after the great mountaineer, conservationist and naturalist, John Muir.

The History

THIS LAND, ITS PLACE names and legends, is replete with ghosts of many of those who came before. However, old campsites and an occasional artifact found along Mono Creek and in the area to the west are the only reminders of the original human visitors, the Indians. Because of the severe winter snows, the area of *Mt. Abbot* quad was not a year-round home for the Miwok and Monache Indians. Instead, these simple people hunted and fished the upland meadows and flats during the warm summer months, and migrated west with the coming of cold weather. Mono Hot Springs (just beyond the west boundary of the quad) was a regularly visited spa used by both the Monache and their tribal cousins to the east, the Paiutes. Using the obvious Mono Pass/Mono Creek trans-Sierra route, these Indians traded back and forth for many years before the coming of the white man, and artifacts left by them in their passing are still being found. It remains a puzzle that the place names of this region ignore the Indian, and instead honor latter-day commercial giants. (Even Lake of the Lone Indian was not, as it would appear, a place name derived from or in honor of these original peoples. Rather, it was named by J. S. Hutchinson, a Sierra Clubber, for the semblance of an Indian profile etched in lichens which he observed on a peak just south of the lake.)

The first white men to visit the western watershed of the San Joaquin River were Spaniards. In 1806 Gabriel

Moraga penetrated an unknown distance up the lower reaches of the San Joaquin River basin on an exploratory expedition. This expedition was followed by a trapping expedition in 1832-1833 led by an American, Ewing Young. Like Moraga, it is unknown how far up the San Joaquin River drainage Young went. Ten years later John Fremont, the famous "Pathfinder," crossed the lower San Joaquin River en route to an unsuccessful attempted crossing of the Sierra via the North Fork of the Kings River. Other than the Moraga expedition, there are no reports of encounters with the Indians of this section of the western slope.

However, the next recorded visit to this region was by a U. S. military patrol in search of a marauding band of Paiutes. This patrol came from the east, over Mono Pass. One year later, in 1864, the noncommissioned officer who directed that patrol led the famous Brewer Survey Party across this same pass to Mono Creek, and thence down to the meadowlands later named Vermilion Valley. This party included William Brewer, Clarence King, James Gardiner and Charles Hoffman. Photographs taken of this adventurous band reveal one common characteristic that contributed to their outstanding list of Sierra firsts: they were obviously in the finest of physical condition. This official survey party, under the direction of State Geologist J. D. Whitney, performed their assigned tasks admirably, and took time from their duties to perform many athletic mountaineering feats. Using the meadows of Vermilion Valley as a base camp, they ventured south for an attempted climb of Mt. Goddard. Using their typical "frontal assault" technique, they failed by a mere 300 feet, and returned exhausted to their camp. No mention is made in their accounts of any local contacts with Indians. If there had been contact, this tired and sweaty crew would most certainly have taken advantage of nearby Mono Hot Springs.

One can assume that prospectors searching for gold penetrated into the area of the *Mt. Abbot* quad during the 1850's and 60's, but there are no written accounts to verify their presence. The Brewer party did encounter one such group to the south, and the later-revealed extent of these miners' high-country ramblings has amazed present-day mountaineers. Similarly, the era of the sheepherder is virtually an unrecorded occupation. Accounts in San Joaquin Valley newspapers occasionally mention these stockmen—usually having to do with sensational murders. There are accounts of range battles that ended up in litigation. However, more often than not these arguments were settled "out of court" by Judge Colt. Graveyard Meadows, just north of Mono Creek, is a case in point: it derives its name from two unmarked graves that are assumed to be those of two sheepherders who lost a "judgment."

The last quarter of the 19th Century in this area is a history of mountaineers. Retracing the steps of the 1864 Brewer Survey party, John Muir skirted the west side of the quad in 1873. The next mountaineers of note were

Theodore Solomons, Joseph Le Conte and Walter Starr, all charter members of the then-new Sierra Club. In 1894 Solomons visited and named Vermilion Valley. From Vermilion Valley, he and his companions, Leigh Bierce (son of Ambrose Bierce), crossed Bear Ridge and ascended Bear Creek, whence they climbed and named Seven Gables Peak. An early snowstorm (September) and a near disaster from a falling tree drove them from the peak, but not before they had had a good look at the rugged country to the south. Solomons, acting on that glimpse of the terrain and a dream nurtured since he was a stripling, decided to investigate the idea of a north-south route between Yosemite and Kings Canyon. The following year (1895) he and Ernest Bonner set out from Yosemite. Their route paralleled the present-day John Muir Trail route to Mono Creek, being farther west. Thence they crossed Bear Ridge and worked their way up the Bear Creek drainage. They then crossed Senger Pass and traveled up the South Fork of the San Joaquin River to Evolution Valley. At this point they elected to take a more westerly direction that took them over the rugged Goddard Divide and Monarch Divide to the South Fork of the Kings, where they concluded a saga that predated the John Muir Trail route by a quarter of a century.

Solomons, in his writings, made mention of the hordes of sheep he had encountered. But it was not until the turn of the century that the destruction these animals wrought on the high-country meadows forced the government to recognize its responsibility by making the area a preserve. In 1893 President Harrison put this area under the aegis of the Sierra Forest Preserve, which regulated the number of horses and cattle that could use the land, and excluded sheep entirely. Muir, who had passed through the country 20 years earlier, was delighted. His reaction to these "hoofed locusts" was, "To let sheep trample so divinely fine a place seems barbarous!" By 1908 the Preserve's designation was changed to that of a National Forest, and the Forest Service administers the present John Muir Wilderness Area.

But today it is not the "hoofed locusts" who threaten this land. Today the threat is man and the automobile. The John Muir Trail now traverses 212 miles of almost uninterrupted wilderness, and today man, in his folly, contemplates breaking this natural primitive stretch with another trans-Sierra highway. Were Muir alive today, he would denounce the crass, materialistic motives of the road's backers in no uncertain terms. He would remind us of our natural heritage and our responsibility to protect it. Only now, he would point out, is the land recovering from the plague of the flocks of sheep. How much time would pass, he would ask, before the grass could break the concrete after man realized his error? How long before the animals that survived would return? How long before the trees that fell before the saw and the bulldozer would reseed and hold back the helpless soil? Humans, he would conclude, need a natural point of reference to lend meaning to their lives, and these ever-narrowing green areas fill that need.

The Geology

MAN IS A TIME-haunted creature. He reckons carefully the expenditure of each passing moment. He is a slave to the time clock, wrist watch, calendar, schedule, deadline and the grave. His vocabulary is filled with words and phrases that utilize the word "time," and yet man, be he physicist or poet, does not know the meaning of the word. How meaningful, for example, is it to state that the rocks of the earth are about 6 billion years old; or that the great Sierra block began rising from an arm of the Pacific Ocean 150 million years ago; or that God created the earth and its biota in 6 "days"? Certainly time involves change, but the unit of measurement used to assess the change has no meaning *other than perspective*. The story the rocks have to tell has valid interest and utility for man because it helps to place him in a

> "Speak to the earth, and it shall teach thee."
> *Job* 12:8

natural frame of reference.

The *Mt. Abbot* quad has rocks that are among the most easily read in the Sierra. Because this section of the western slope is part of the least faulted and most cohesive stretch of the great Sierran block, its chapters have been avidly studied by geologists. Like the Yosemite region to the north, most of the country has been extensively and repeatedly glaciated, and this glaciation has uncovered the Sierra batholith, a great granite dome 11-14 miles thick which, until the glaciation, lay below the surface sediments of ancient seas. In perspective, this period of glaciation was recent, but it was these rivers of ice that sculpted and carved the deep U-shaped valleys that are now the watersheds of Mono Creek, Bear Creek and the South Fork of the San Joaquin. That section of Fish Creek shown on this topo map was in the uppermost reaches of the Fish Creek glacier—a typical, large, shallow cirque basin.

At times, each of the watersheds named above held a separate and distinct glacier—a moving mass of ice 15 or 20 miles long. However, at one point the Bear Creek glacier did "overflow" its banks and join the *mer de glace* (sea of ice) that occupied the Mono Creek watershed. This "overflow" occurred at the point where the Bear Creek glacier made its right-angle turn west-

---

"A thousand years in thy sight are but as yesterday when it is past, and as a watch in the night."
Psalms XC:4

---

ward. The ice river then covered Bear Ridge, the junction occurring near the present route of the John Muir Trail. All these glacial tributaries contributed to the 1500-square-mile San Joaquin glacier system, and each, with the exception of the Bear Creek glacier, originated in a cirque that nestled against the main Sierra crest. The Bear Creek glacier began from the unnamed divide topped by Mt. Hooper and Mt. Senger.

Today's visitor to this region of glaciated country should know some of the rudiments of a glacier's dynamics, for it is out of this understanding that many of the landforms and peculiarities of terrain take on meaning and interest. A glacier is indeed a river of ice, complete with eddies and currents. The flow is, of course, much slower, but in measuring time, speed is a relative factor. The bottom and sides of the glacial current serve as the working agents of erosion. Here rocks frozen into the ice "sandpaper" the underlying rock surfaces, and large blocks of rock which have been "plucked" from the rock floor "bound and tumble" in the glacial "current." As contributing glacial systems enter the main mass, it expands, and the current widens and slows down. The sheer mass and weight of the moving ice has enormous erosive power—in the case of the San Joaquin glacier system, it wore away entire mountain spurs. The deepest areas of glacial erosion occur where there is the least resistance, in areas of softer rock and rock that is highly jointed (seamed).

When the ice finally receded after several million years of ebb and flow, its course was marked by a U-shaped valley that had been plucked, scraped and scoured from the hard granite of the Sierra batholith. Contributing glaciers with less mass than the main glacier carved less deep valleys, and these were left "high and dry" on the main valley's wall. Geologists call these "hanging valleys." It should be remembered that glacial systems, like stream systems, are dendritic (like a tree, with many twigs and branches feeding into a trunk) and that hanging valleys have, in turn, hanging valleys of their own. In the Mono glacier system, one can readily see this phenomenon in the Recesses and in the Grinnell and Pioneer Basin tributaries.

As the dynamics of a glacier's active, growing flow are important, so also is its recession. Stones varying in size from a grain of sand to hunks twice the size of a house are left at the foot and along the sides of the glacier. Aggregations of these, geologists are pleased to call *moraines* and *outwash*. The ebbing and flowing of the glaciers leave a conflicting story of moraines, but the general effect remaining is that a glaciated valley has morainal shoulders along its sides and morainal dikes extending across the valley floor. Many of the latter have been subsequently cut and given a V-shaped cross section by river flow. Typically, these moraines are made up of sand, silt, and rounded boulders. An occasional huge, rounded boulder is left isolated from the rest, and this landmark is called an "erratic." Lastly, the "sand-papering" by silt and boulders leaves, as token of its work, *glacial polish* (slick rock surfaces) and *striae* (longitudinal scratches) on the more resistant rock of the valley floor and walls. Fine examples of moraines can be seen around Lake Thomas A. Edison and on the surrounding uplands above Mono Creek.

The Flora

NATURAL PHENOMENA are irrevocably bound together, and the flora and fauna of this quad are, as they are everywhere in the High Sierra, a contingent of this period of glaciation. For example, moraines later serve as natural dams. Lakes form behind the moraines, and slowly they fill with sediment. This sediment, in turn, serves as a root culture for meadow grasses and trees. (In the instances of Lake Thomas A. Edison and Florence Lake, man has reversed this process by building dams. The waters behind these dams now cover the once meadow-filled floor of Vermilion Valley, and the once-grassy fringe of then-tiny Florence Lake.) This process is still going on, and many areas like what used to be Kip Camp on Bear Creek have had their open meadow portions almost overrun by lodgepole pines. The upper cirque basins—areas of the most recent and repeated glaciation—are today the best examples of alpine and subalpine meadows. Here, fewer plants—and thus fewer animals—will be found. Because of their relatively short growing season, these plants are mostly of the sedge family, color here being provided by a few stunted perennials.

> "Where flowers degenerate man cannot live."
> Napoleon

The conifers and deciduous trees that blanket sections

of *Mt. Abbot* quad are of 4 life zones: the Transition (2500'-8000'), the Canadian (8000'-10000'), the Hudsonian (9000'-11000') and the Arctic-Alpine (10300'—). The areas of the Transition and Canadian zones are found almost exclusively in the valley troughs and on the morainal shoulders, where sands, sediments and decayed rock offer a rooting foothold for trees. Among the trees found in the Transition zone are yellow pine (ponderosa), incense cedar, sugar pine, Douglas fir, white fir, black cottonwood and black oak. Most of the trails described here travel through the cooler uplands of the Canadian zone. With the exception of a few moisture-seeking birch and quaking aspen, these uplands are exclusively the province of conifers like lodgepole pine, red fir and Jeffrey pine.

The ubiquitous lodgepole pine carries over onto the next elevational step, the Hudsonian zone, and travelers working their way up the western slope will find the lodgepole's distinctive 2-needle clustered branchlets next to gracefully nodding sprays of the mountain hemlock. Near timberline, the 5-needled whitebark pine is the solitary sentinel of the high country, and its arms-uplifted silhouette signals to the climber that open high country lies just ahead.

Somehow it is always this harsh, open, high country that mountaineers talk about when they exchange experiences around a campfire. Known as the Arctic-Alpine Belt, it is that rocky region above timberline where visitors can shiver in the cold wind and simultaneously acquire a severe sunburn. Life here exists on the brink of survival, and time is condensed into a mere 7-9-week growing season. Plant growth is restricted to those scarce footholds of soil provided by shallow alpine cirques, sink-basins, and rock crevices. Despite this difficult environment, more than 40 species of grasses, sedges and wildflowers grow here, and their rush to complete their propagation within their allotted time seems irrepressibly boisterous.

Here joyful color is provided by red, yellow and magenta Indian paintbrush, scarlet gilia, rose-purple heather, white phlox, sky-blue polemonium, rose-red pentstemon and magenta-hued Sierra primrose. Alpine lakes dot cirque floors, seeming at first glance to be entirely rockbound, but a closer look reveals tiny, grassy pockets—each with its own private garden. Even where there appears to be no soil at all, one finds spotty clumps of plants clinging tenuously to cracks in the rock, their roots stretching deep. Hikers and packers traveling the trails of the Silver Divide and the headwaters of Hilgard Creek and the East Fork of Bear Creek will encounter these plants, and when they do, they will feel the almost tangible will to survive that infuses growing things in these harsh climes.

The Fauna

LIKE THE PLANTS, the animals of the Alpine Belt are scarce, hardy, and adapted to the short summers of plenty. The spawning season for the fishes is almost prohibitively short, but specimens like the native (to the Sierra) golden trout and the imported eastern brook trout seem ideally suited to the cold waters of high-country lakes and tarns, and they are plentiful in this quad. One can properly wonder how the abundant fish populations of these rocky regions manage to get enough food. Because soil is rare, and rich, loamy, overhung banks are characteristic of waters at lower elevations, these trout depend heavily on wind-borne insects. It has been estimated that there are over 10,000 different insects in the Sierra —but the back-country traveler knows that the estimator was simply counting the mosquitoes around his campfire.

It is an unfortunate fact that these same winds, generally from the west, are also bringing deadly insecticides used in the San Joaquin Valley. Recent investigations have shown that some of these high-country trout, even those in lakes above 10,000′, are accumulating these poisons in their fatty tissues. DDT, in particular, is showing a marked rise in the fatty tissues of sampled trout and frogs of this region (DDT is soluble in fat, but not in water), and although these poisons have not reached dangerous levels for human consumption, man must begin to check the threat before, not after, that level is reached.

Wild animal sightings are always exciting events, and water margins are always likely places from which to make them. A campsite located within sight of a tarn or lake in the Alpine Belt is a good place to watch the evening parade of animals as they come to water. Conies, tiny rabbit-like hay gatherers, rarely come to drink, but their industrious harvesting of grasses and other alpine plants makes them a frequent visitor to the grassy pockets on the lake's shoreline. More often than not, however, the camper will hear a cony's high, nasal *keck-eck* before actually seeing the animal. Another animal that likes the water edges is the Aplodontia. This little rodent with the name like a dental plate is about twice the size of the cony, and looks like an overlarge meadow mouse—without the tail. A burrowing animal, he prefers streamside areas for his runways, and the entrances to his tunnels are clearly marked by much fresh-cut vegetation.

The largest grass-foraging mammal resident of the Alpine Belt is the marmot. Sometimes as long as 2 feet, this chunky member of the ground-squirrel tribe is easily identified. He is a lover of rocky terrain, and talus slopes are a marmot Eden. Marmots residing near high-country trails never quite get used to the traffic, but if the hiker or rider continues on by at a normal pace, the marmot will often not rise from his daily sun bath but will merely watch until the tolerated visitor is well past. When alarmed, he sounds a shrill whistle and runs for his burrow. Because he has more than the usual amount of curiosity, he can't stay down in his burrow long, and the hiker with a little patience will be rewarded by a glimpse of a black face emerging from underneath a rock. He and his family (the young emerge from the burrow in July) are often seen in the early evening as they come to water to drink.

Lakes with meadowed inlets or outlets are fine places from which to make sightings of the Belding ground squirrel (up to 12,000'). Also known as the "picketpin" because of his resemblance to that particular item in a packer's hardware, he assumes an alert, upright stance at the first intimation of danger—the better to see across the meadow grasses—and emits a series of shrill, short whistles. His whistle is taken up by any other Beldings in the meadow, and a traveler's appearance at a meadow's edge is often a clamorous affair.

Near the high meadows, generally back among the fallen timber, is found the alpine chipmunk. Like the related ground squirrel, this chipmunk has cheek pouches into which he stuffs seeds, nuts, berries, camp leftovers and an occasional insect. He is the smallest of the Sierra chipmunks and the least colorfully marked: alternately dark and light stripes on the back, with light tan sides and tail. The alpine chipmunk is a staple in the diet of the high country's carnivores, as are the other animals described above.

But carnivores are rare in the high country, and the back-country traveler can count himself lucky if he makes a sighting of a marten, a weasel, a red fox or a mountain coyote. The red-tailed hawk and the great horned owl are more commonly seen, but even they are scarce. In all likelihood the nearest one will come to these animals is the indelible story of an opened burrow, or an evening serenade by either the owl or a couple of sorrowful coyotes.

As the number of carnivores found in the Alpine Belt is restricted, so too is the birdlife. At and just above timberline the most distinctive and readily identified bird is the Clark nutcracker. In his clearly delineated black and white plumage, he is usually seen perched in the top of a whitebark pine. He is a typically crass member of the crow family, and his raucous cawing echoes about the rock environs of the high country. By contrast, the rosy finch is quite sedate. This flittering resident of snow-covered passes is often the only company of the solitary mountaineer, and his tuneless chirp is usually recalled with fond nostalgia. Other representatives of alpine bird life include the pine grosbeak, the three-toed woodpecker, and, as mentioned, the great horned owl and the red-tailed hawk.

The Climate

BIRD WATCHERS, who spend a good deal of their wilderness time staring up toward the skies, are among the first of a party to be aware of a change in the weather. Summer storms, usually of the afternoon-shower variety, are not uncommon in the Sierra, and they are usually preceded by a cumulus cloud buildup. (Storms of longer duration generally follow several days of high overcast.) Keeping a "weather eye peeled" is not a phrase restricted to the nautical fraternity, and back-country travelers who utilize breaks in the forest canopy to study weather developments are well on their way to becoming creditable woodsmen.

Besides the utilitarian benefits that accrue to sky-watchers, there is the esthetic opportunity of watching

"Small showers last long, but sudden storms are short.   Shakespeare, *Richard II*

the total spectacle of a storm—a chance of increasing rarity in today's city canyons.

If one is lucky, he will one day find himself, under a secure shelter, in the high country where he can watch the birth of harmless white puffs of cloud. In an amazingly short time these tiny powderpuffs grow until they are towering giants with dark, threatening bases. Soon they crowd the blue into narrow strips, and from several of the cloud's dark bases one can see the rain descend in a short, black veil. Often the veil of rain is bent at its base by driving winds, and by simple deduction one can determine the direction of the storm. If one has a map handy and knows some of the landmarks, he can even ascertain the approximate speed. Jagged streaks of lightning then appear, seeming at first to make a random pattern. The boom of thunder that attends each strike sounds to the distant watcher like a dull rumble, and the time the sound takes to arrive seems ponderously long. But as the storm nears, the booms become distinct, and the observer can see that most of the lightning strikes are emanating from the periphery of the storm. The rain veil no longer appears bent, and soon the lightning and thunder are upon the watcher. A nearby lodgepole pine with a dead top is struck, and as the moisture in the tree is instantly vaporized, the tree-top explodes. The crack of the thunder is instantaneous as the edge of the storm passes, and each earth-jarring crack is an oppressive force that one can feel in his stomach.

Then comes the rain. Only a few drops at first, and then it picks up force as the wind catches it and sweeps it across the ground. As the storm passes there is another brief flurry of lightning strikes, and then the thunderous cracks diminish to a dull rumble. Overhead a break between the clouds admits some welcome sunshine, and the watcher emerges to the fragrance of wet pine humus and a newly cleansed world.

Despite the beauty of a high-country thunder shower,

most travelers would prefer dry weather for the duration of their wilderness stay. And the odds are that they will not see rain, for the summer-season percentage of total yearly precipitation in this part of the country is merely 3%. Still, in the interests of peace of mind (and keeping dry) most summer back-country travelers carry some kind of a minimum shelter (tube tent, plastic tarp).

For the most part, the summertime temperatures of *Mt. Abbot* quad are quite comfortable, but the differences between those near Lake Thomas A. Edison and those around Lake Italy can be as much as 30 degrees. (The rule of thumb for estimating elevational temperature differences is that the temperature decreases by 1° F. for each 300-foot rise). One can usually count on summer maximum temperatures in the lower elevations of the quad of about 70°-80° F., and in the higher elevations of 50°-60° F. These temperatures are lower at night, the coldest time being between 3 and 6 a.m., and after a rainstorm. Winter years which leave large high-country snowpacks tend to make for colder summers, particularly if the snow remains year-round.

The Trails

THE BEST-KNOWN trail in this quad is the famous *John Muir Trail,* which bisects the quad on a northwest-to-southeast line. Of the whole 212 miles of the Muir Trail, the part described here runs from Tully Hole in the north to Sally Keyes Lakes in the south. Other main trails described here are the *Mono Creek/Mono Pass* trail (described from Vermilion Campground to Mosquito Flat Roadend), and the *Bear Creek/Italy Pass* trail (described from the Bear Creek Diversion Dam Jeep Road Junction to the Pine Creek Roadend). The east-side access lateral over *McGee Pass* is described from the McGee Creek Roadend to the junction with the John Muir Trail. Laterals and cross-country routes also described include *Fish Creek* to *Mono Creek* via Red and White Lake and Grinnell Lake, the *loop from Rosemarie Meadow to Marie Lake* via Sandpiper Lake and the *circuit of the Gemini and Pinnacles* formations.

For the hiker with the experience, stamina and desire, the east half of *Mt. Abbot* quad is great country for some do-it-yourself cross-country explorations. All the tributaries of Mono Creek except the North Fork are trailless in their upper reaches, and the seeker of solitude will almost certainly find it at, say, upper Pioneer Basin or Lower Mills Creek Lake. There are even not-too-difficult ways out of the Mono Creek drainage at the heads of Pioneer Basin, Hopkins Creek and Mills Creek. Farther south, the route from French Canyon to Merriam Lakes is a moderately difficult path to a surpassingly beautiful alpine setting.

The Trailheads

THERE ARE SIX major trailheads giving access to the country of the *Mt. Abbot* quadrangle: **Vermilion Campground, Bear Diversion Dam Jeep Road Junction, Mosquito Flat, Pine Creek Roadend, McGee Creek Roadend, Florence Lake.** Only Florence Lake and the Jeep Road Junction are actually on the *Mt. Abbot* map, but Vermilion Campground and Mosquito Flat are only a mile or so off the map.

HAIKU

"Seek on high bare trails
Sky-reflecting
Violets . . .
Mountain top jewels."

Basho

VERMILION CAMPGROUND (7650′)

Reached by:

Auto from Fresno or Madera via hiways 145, 168 for 72 miles to Huntington Lake and then 26 miles on a surfaced road to Lake Thomas A. Edison. Boat-taxi service is usually available to the upper end of the lake.

Access to: (mileages from the campground)

Mono Creek, 6-16 miles

John Muir Trail, 6 miles

BEAR DIVERSION DAM JEEP ROAD JUNCTION (7000')

Reached by:
Auto from Fresno or Madera as above, stopping at the junction about one mile north of Mono Hot Springs.

Access to:
John Muir Trail, 9 miles
Lake Italy, 18 miles
Marie Lake, 16 miles

MOSQUITO FLAT (10250')

Reached by:
Auto from hiway 395 at Tom's Place, 24 miles north of Bishop, and then 11 miles by oiled road to Little Lakes Valley. Bus service is available to Tom's Place.

Access to:
Mono Creek, 6-16 miles
Grinnell Lakes, 15 miles
Pioneer Basin, 9-11 miles
Mono Creek Recesses, 7-16 miles
Hopkins Lakes, 11-14 miles

PINE CREEK ROADEND (7580')

Reached by:
Auto from hiway 395. Turn west at a junction 10

miles northwest of Bishop and go 10 miles up a paved road.

Access to:
Lake Italy, 11 miles
John Muir Trail, 18 miles

McGEE CREEK ROADEND (8300′)

Reached by:
Auto from hiway 395 opposite Lake Crowley, 4 miles up a dirt road.

Access to:
John Muir Trail in Tully Hole, 13 miles
Grinnell Lakes, 14 miles

FLORENCE LAKE (7350′)

Reached by:
Auto from Madera or Fresno via hiways 145, 168 (93 miles from Fresno). Boats usually available to upper end of lake.

Access to: (mileages from upper lake)
Junction John Muir Trail, northbound, 7 miles

CAMPGROUNDS NEAR THE TRAILHEADS

NEAREST VERMILION CAMPGROUND AND BEAR DIVERSION DAM JEEP ROAD JUNCTION

Vermilion Campground (7650′). 30 sites.

Mono Hot Springs (6500'). 3 miles north of the Lake Edison/Florence Lake "Y". Hot springs resort nearby, with post office, restaurant, gas and supplies. 32 sites.

Mono Creek (7400'). 3 miles north of Mono Hot Springs. 20 sites.

NEAREST MOSQUITO FLAT

Mosquito Flat (10250'). Near the roadend in Little Lakes Valley. Supplies at Rock Creek Resort nearby. 10 sites, parking lot.

Rock Creek Lake (9600'). 10 miles south of hiway 395 on paved road. Supplies at Rock Creek Resort nearby. 24 sites at inlet, 18 sites at outlet.

NEAREST PINE CREEK ROADEND

Roadend. There are no formal campgrounds at the Pine Creek Roadend, but sometimes backpackers have found a place to sleep, and there is some parking space.

Horton Creek (5000'). 7 miles NW of Bishop, via hiway 395, and 4 miles up Round Valley Road. 53 sites.

NEAREST McGEE CREEK ROADEND

McGee Creek (7600'). 2 miles west of hiway 395 opposite Crowley Lake on dirt road. 16 sites. Supplies at McGee Creek resort.

NEAREST FLORENCE LAKE

Florence Lake (7350′). 22 miles east of Huntington Lake at the north end of Florence Lake. Supplies, boat rental, ferryboat service at nearby resort. 12 sites.

Jackass Meadow (7200′). 22 miles east of Huntington Lake near the north end of Florence Lake. Supplies etc. as above. 7 sites.

Trail Descriptions

Main Trail #1 (John Muir Trail): This 28-mile segment of the Sierra's most famous pathway, the John Muir Trail, is here described from Tully Hole (just off the north boundary of the quad) to Sally Keyes Lakes. This description is continued (on the north) in the High Sierra Hiking Guide to *Devils Postpile* and (on the south) in the High Sierra Hiking Guide to *Blackcap Mountain.*

The trail leaves Tully Hole by a gentle descent. From the trail, the traveler has splendid views and access to the numerous small falls and holes that characterize nearby Fish Creek. Where the trail crests the rocky ridge above the head of Cascade Valley, there are good views across the valley to the Silver Divide. As the trail switchbacks down, the muted roar of now-tumbling Fish Creek sounds from the left, and the hiker gets a parting glimpse of this memorable stream's last plunge when crossing the bridge at the foot of the descent. The trail then passes the junction with the Cascade Valley trail and climbs steeply over a densely forested slope on the east side of the outlet stream from Helen Lake. Midway up this climb the trail passes several campsites situated in a picturesque meadow on the right (west), and then begins the final, long, steep climb to Helen Lake. This section of trail is rocky and eroded as it passes through a spectrum of changing timber cover: silver pine and lodgepole, concentrations of mountain hemlock and, finally, thinning lodgepole. From the final switchbacks just below Helen Lake, the trail affords instructive views of the U-shaped glacial valley that the route has traversed.

As the trail tops the granite brink of the cirque containing tiny Helen Lake (a sign at the lake and the Department of Fish and Game call this lake "Squaw Lake") the traveler is struck with the awesome scale of the ice mass that began here and in the nearby cirque (containing Bobs Lake) about ½ mile over the steep granite slope to the southeast. The trail rock-hops across the outlet of Helen Lake, veers westerly past two small tarns, and then passes the Goodale Pass turnoff as it veers south to Warrior Lake. From the north shore of this lake, the trail ascends by steep, rocky switchbacks to the top of the Silver Divide (Silver Pass, 10900′).

The views from this colorful pass continue as the trail descends on the south side above Silver Pass Lake.

The Ant

"The ant has made himself illustrious
Through constant industry industrious.
    So what?
Would you be calm and placid
If you were full of formic acid?"

                                    Ogden Nash

Rounding the grassy shores of this alpine jewel, the trail hangs on the rocky slopes above the outlet creek for a short distance, and then drops steeply to the ford. Continuing south on the west side of the stream, the trail re-enters a sparse forest cover of lodgepole pine before dropping steeply into the North Fork of Mono Creek drainage. Midway down this descent the trail refords the outlet of Silver Pass Lake, and then fords the North Fork. Passing an unmaintained trail to Mott Lake, the trail stays on the east side of the creek on a steady descent through an increasingly dense forest cover. This descent then meets and joins the main Mono Creek/Mono Pass trail, and our route goes right (west) toward Quail Meadows.

A short distance beyond this junction, the trail refords the North Fork, and then it levels as it reaches the dense forest fringes of Quail Meadows (7760′). At the eastern edge of this flat, our route branches left (south), leaving the Mono Creek/Mono Pass trail. At this writing, a steel bridge was scheduled to supplant a long and sometimes hazardous ford of the creek. After the ford, the trail begins the long, steep, rocky climb over Bear Ridge. In 2 steps this ascent stepladders up by steady switchbacks over glacial till left by both the Mono Creek and Bear Creek glaciers. The crown of Bear Ridge (10000′) affords excellent views of Volcanic Knob to the east, the only vulcan outcropping in the quad, before beginning the steep descent to Bear Creek. The forest cover of lodgepole pine and Sierra juniper becomes denser with the descent, and by the time the trail passes the stock-drift fence just above what used to be Kip Camp, it is lined by red-fir stands. A sand flat situated in the midst of a mixed forest cover of lodgepole, juniper, red fir and quaking aspen marks the junction with the Bear Creek/Italy Pass main trail.

Continuing south, our route then ascends moderately along the northeast banks of Bear Creek, and passes several improved packer campsites situated near large, log-jammed pools in the river. We then pass the Italy Pass trail and by footlog ford several branchlets of Hilgard Creek. Near these wetter sections of trail, one will find abundant whorled blue-purple pentstemon, yellow and purple shooting star, prickly red gooseberry and yellow wallflower. The ascent is still gentle-to-moderate as it passes several more improved campsites between open granite slab sections with meadowy breaks, and arrives at the trail junction where the Vee and Seven Gables lakes trail branches left (east). This junction is just a few yards short of the Bear Creek ford—a wade-across ford that is hazardous during high water. Those on foot will find the going easier by using the footlog ford ⅛ mile downstream (due west of the last improved packer campsite). After fording the stream via this footlog, one rejoins our route at the west side of the wade-across ford cited above via a short section of the Orchid Lake trail. The trail then ascends steeply by switchbacks to the corduroy-bridge crossing of the West Fork of Bear Creek at Rosemarie Meadow and the junction of the Lou Beverly/Sandpiper Lakes trail. After crossing the West Fork of Bear Creek, the trail climbs steeply above timberline and arrives at the alpine meadows surrounding Marie Lake. Keeping to the west side of the lake, our route passes tiny clumps of stunted hemlock and lodgepole pine and a ground cover of heather, lousewort and western mountain aster. From the south end of the lake, the trail ascends on a moderate-to-steep grade to Selden Pass (10873'). Breather stops on this climb offer fine views back to Mt. Hilgard and the granitoid Marie Lake cirque. From Selden Pass the trail descends over short, steep switchbacks to Heart Lake. This rockbound, heart-shaped lake has a meadow-turfed fringe delicately colored with heather, primrose and yellow columbine. Angling for golden trout makes this lake an interesting rest stop. Nonfishermen will find sampling the views a fine way to pass the time. From the outlet, one can see Mts. Goddard and Henry to the southeast. To the southwest Ward Mtn. and Mt. Shinn are the most prominent peaks. Continuing the moderate descent from Heart Lake along its outlet stream, the trail arrives at Sally Keyes Lakes. This short walk is lined with an abundance of wildflowers including corn lily, Indian paintbrush, Douglas phlox, shooting star, yellow cinquefoil, milfoil, pentstemon, lupine, red heather, wallflower, nude buckwheat and western mountain aster. Some backpackers claim Sally Keyes Lakes are warm enough for more or less comfortable swimming.

Main Trail #2 (Mono Crk./Mono Pass). This 22-mile main trail follows the ancient Indian trading route down the Mono Creek valley. The trailheads at either end of the trail are situated less than 1 mile from the east and west boundaries of the *Mt. Abbot* quad, and though the description below follows an east-to-west course using the eastern starting point of Mosquito Flat, one can as well start from the western trailhead at Vermilion Campground. Either way takes the angler along 8 trout-filled miles of Mono Creek, with rainbow, golden, brook and brown trout.

Mosquito Flat (10400′) marks the edge of the John Muir Wilderness Area (no motorized vehicles). Our trail starts southwest, passes the 1-mile lateral to Eastern Brook Lakes, and crosses a low, rocky ridge to the west side of Mack Lake. Here our route leaves the Little Lakes Valley trail and branches right toward Mono Pass. Our trail then ascends steeply via some rather rocky switchbacks. The forest cover is moderately dense stands of whitebark and lodgepole pine along a rocky slope. Views from this slope are excellent—even superb —both of the Little Lakes Valley and of the Sierra Nevada crest. The majestic skyline includes six landmark peaks, all over 13000 feet, and three glaciers. The peaks are Mt. Mills (13468′), Mt. Abbot (13715′), Mt. Dade (13600+′), Mt. Julius Caesar (13196′), Bear Creek Spire (13713′) and Mt. Morgan (13748′).

From the cirque formed by these peaks the main glacier flowed northeast in the direction of the present flow of Rock Creek, and the direction of our trail parallels the feeder glacier that emanated from the Ruby Lake cirque. As the trail crosses the meadow just below Ruby Lake, it nears the outlet creek from the lake (11100′). The sheer granite walls of this cirque tower 1500′ and more above the lake surface, and their crest on the west side is a series of spectacular pinnacles. To the north the low notch marks Mono Pass, and from the lake one can watch the antlike progress of pack trains and backpackers as they switchback up the precipitous, barren talus of the south ridge of Mt. Starr.

From Ruby Lake the trail ascends steeply over the rocky switchbacks on the south slope of Mt. Starr to Mono Pass (12,000′), a notch in the cirque wall just west of Mt. Starr. Views from the pass are excellent, but those wishing a panoramic outlook on the spectacular Sierra crest should ascend the granite shoulder of Mt. Starr, an easy climb to the east. From this vantage point one has a complete perspective of Pioneer Basin and Mts. Stanford, Huntington, Crocker and Hopkins, and Red and White Mountain to the north. To the south one has "end-on" views of Mts. Abbot and Dade, Bear Creek Spire, and Mt. Humphreys.

From Mono Pass the trail descends over granite slopes past barren Summit Lake, and then drops more severely as it veers westerly above Trail Lake. This route then turns northward and fords Golden Creek.

Following the north side of the stream in a moderately dense forest cover, the trail passes by the lateral to

Fourth Recess Lake, a favorite "off the beaten track" campsite. Our route continues to descend, fording the outlet streams from Pioneer Basin and paralleling the westward course of Mono Creek. As the Mono Creek

> "Luck affects everything; let your hook always be cast; in the stream where you least expect it there will be a fish."   **Ovid.**

Valley opens up beyond Mono Rock, the trail passes by the steep lateral to Third Recess Lake and, about a mile farther, descends past the turnoff to Lower Hopkins Lake and the Hopkins Lake basin. In late season the groves of quaking aspen that line the stream's banks are a colorful backdrop to an otherwise steady conifer green. Owing to heavy traffic, this segment of trail becomes dusty where it passes the Grinnell Lake lateral and descends to Fish Camp (8500'). This traditional camping place marks the junction of the Mono Creek trail with the Second Recess lateral, and travelers will find good campsites (Forest Service "Improved") on both the north and south sides of the creek (access to the latter via a bridge).

As this route descends along the north side of Mono Creek past the aspen groves, the traveler occasionally has views of the stern northern face of Volcanic Knob to the south; and from several spots along the trail one looks up the long, chutelike valley of the First Recess to the granite-topped heights of Recess Peak. About 2½ miles below Fish Camp the trail turns right, away from the narrowing canyon, and climbs by rocky switchbacks to the crown of a ridge, where it joins the John Muir Trail. Thence it descends a short distance on the east side of the North Fork of Mono Creek, and fords the

> "Some circumstantial evidence is very strong, as when you find a trout in the milk." Thoreau

North Fork just above its confluence with Mono Creek. From the ford to the edge of Quail Meadows is a gentle downhill walk through dense forest cover. At Quail Meadows the John Muir Trail branches left (south) and fords Mono Creek.

Our route leaves the John Muir Trail at Quail Meadows and proceeds westerly on a level stretch. Mono Creek now cascades over a series of granite-bedrocked holes (fine swimming in late season) before flowing into the northeast tip of Lake Edison. This man-made, granite-edged lake dominates the views to the south for the remainder of this trip. A boat-taxi service operates the length of the lake, based at a resort adjoining Vermilion Campground, but advance inquiry should be made about length of operating season and ferry schedule. (Write to High Sierra Resort/Lake Thomas A. Edison/Mono Hot Springs/California 93642.) The ferry lands at the northeast tip of the lake, and the unmarked footpath giving access to this point can be seen from the trail. The newly constructed trail along the upper reaches of the north side of Lake Edison undulates severely over alternately rocky and dusty stretches. At some points the trail crosses granite ridges 600' above the lake surface, and from these ridges the traveler has fine views of heavily timbered Bear Ridge across the lake. The forest cover reflects the lower altitude, as Jeffrey pine and red fir mix with the ever-present lodgepole. This forest becomes quite dense as our route passes the

---

"Hurry is only admirable in catching flies."
Halburton

---

trail going right (north) to Graveyard Meadows and Goodale Pass. A faint trail to the left (south) leads to another landing point, on a nearby bay. Our route continues westward, crosses the bridge over Cold Creek, and passes the trail lateral to Devils Bathtub. Beyond this junction the hiker leaves the worst of the dust behind as the trail winds through a dense stand of Jeffrey pine to the Forest Service access road. This sandy road descends gently to the eastern edge of Vermilion Campground (7650').

Main Trail #3 (Bear Crk./Italy Pass): Although this 30-mile main trail is described from west to east, there is no reason why it should not be traveled in the opposite direction. The western trailhead (7000′) is at the Jeep Road junction (to Bear Diversion Dam) on the Mono Hot Springs/Lake Thomas A. Edison road. This jeep road is impassable to anything but 4-wheel-drive vehicles and foot traffic. As the jeep road leaves the main road, it swings first east and then south, undulating gently as it traverses the long granite field that marks the southeast end of Bear Ridge. Rounding Bear Ridge, the road ascends gently, and then drops down to the Bear Diversion Dam spillway.

At the dam (7350′) the traveler enters the mouth of the canyon whose walls rise steeply on either side of Bear Creek. The trail (unsigned) skirts the west and north sides of the tiny Bear Diversion Dam reservoir and strikes out east-northeast, along the north side of Bear Creek. Soon the canyon walls close in, and the forest cover becomes moderate to dense. Should one desire to try the fishing for brown trout along the stream, he will also more than likely encounter small stands of water-loving cottonwood and aspen en route, as well as some lodgepole, oak, and the first fir on this ascent. Near the creek, wildflower-fanciers will relish the luxuriant growth of pentstemon, lupine, paintbrush, monkey flower, and cinquefoil. Bear Creek, in the stretch immediately above the reservoir, is a rock-bottomed, briskly flowing stream with a surprising penchant for suddenly eddying out into broad, emerald-green pools.

For 1½ miles above the reservoir, the trail ascends very gradually, and then as the canyon narrows it begins to ascend more steeply. The duff trail gives way to rocky underfooting, which prevails for the rest of the trip, and about ½ mile farther this route encounters the signed boundary of the John Muir Wilderness Area. At the boundary, one can catch his first V-notched glimpse of Recess Peak directly up canyon. The trail drops down for a short distance and then begins a steady, rocky ascent. Several good campsites dot the nearby banks of Bear Creek, and the traveler can take his choice of any of these primitives, or continue to ascend to the large packer campsite just below the confluence of Bear Creek and Cirque Creek. Though the emerald-green pools occur less often, they stand in dramatic contrast to the plunging white water, and, understandably, most of the campsites are located beside these stiller sections of water.

In this country slight changes in altitude entail significant changes in the plant and animal life. For example, as the trail ascends steeply to the packer site mentioned above, fishermen find golden trout as well as brown in their catch, and exploring naturalists discover that the predominant forest cover is now Jeffrey pine and the shrubs are now mostly gooseberry and snow brush. Arrival at the packer site is presaged by several "corduroy" bridge crossings of marshy sections, and a stock-drift fence.

The trail then veers away northerly from cascading Bear Creek. As it ascends steadily up the north wall of the canyon, one has good views of the jumbled cirque crest on the opposite side of the canyon to the southeast. Though rocky, this trail is well maintained where it rises above the floor of the valley. The moderate-to-dense forest cover of the creek bottom thins as the trail climbs to the slight granite-ribbed saddle that marks the start of the descent to old Kip Camp and the trail's reunion with Bear Creek. The descent reveals a marked change in the forest cover: the predominant Jeffrey pine of the lower canyon has given way to lodgepole and juniper. Where the views during the ascent were of the down-canyon Bear Creek drainage, the descent brings views of the Mono Divide. Just above old Kip Camp, a bend in the duff trail reveals Mt. Hilgard, and as we near the flats of old Kip Camp we find that the timber now includes red fir. The aspen- and cottonwood-lined banks of Bear Creek reappear on the immediate right as

"Whatsoever thy hand findeth to do, do it with thy might; for there is no work, nor device, nor knowledge, nor wisdom in the grave, whither thou goest."   Ecclesiastes 9:10

our route strikes the John Muir Trail and turns right. Just a few yards to the southeast of the junction is where Kip Camp (8880′) used to be. It has been closed because of overuse.

From old Kip Camp (8880'), the moderately ascending trail stays very close to the east bank of Bear Creek. This ascent soon leaves the flats of old Kip Camp behind, and the forest cover changes to lodgepole. Within 2 miles after leaving the flats, one sees the last of the familiar quaking aspen, and the canyon takes on more of an open valley feeling. Three improved packer campsites (at intervals of about 1 mile) line Bear Creek for the first 3 miles above old Kip Camp, and their presence indicates the heavy use that the Muir trail is subjected to. On the left, below Mt. Hilgard, one can see the Hilgard Creek canyon come into view. At the confluence of Hilgard Creek and Bear Creek, our route branches left (east) from the John Muir Trail. The Hilgard Creek trail ascends steadily through a thinning forest cover of lodgepole and then over large patches of glacially smoothed granite.

Midway between the trail junction and Lake Italy, the trail levels out temporarily, only to begin climbing abruptly via short, rocky switchbacks. High on the left the rocky prominence of Mt. Hilgard dominates the skyline as the switchbacks temporarily end. The trail fords the stream, and then resumes its switchbacking. Just below Teddy Bear Lake, the trail passes timberline, and then crosses long granite ledges that alternate with grassy patches to the outlet of Lake Italy (11150'). This large, bootlike lake derives its name from its similarity to the European peninsula. Rounding the curve of the lake just above the outlet, one can easily see the cirque basin where the feeder glacier had its beginnings. At the east end of the cirque, Bear Creek Spire marks the division between the western and eastern directional flows of the old glaciers. To the west towers Mt. Hilgard; to the north, Mt. Gabb; and to the east are Bear Creek Spire and Mt. Julius Caesar. To the immediate north of Bear Creek Spire, filling the distant skyline, are Mts. Dade, Abbot and Mills. A climber's heaven: every peak bordering this lake towers well over 13000'.

Our route rounds the southern edge of the lake, and ascends to the rocky hanging valley occupied by Jumble Lake. This route skirts the north side of the lake and climbs steeply to Italy Pass (12300'), where the views to the north are dominated by Mt. Julius Caesar. Ahead, to the east, we can see the unusual, unnamed, chocolate layer-cake mountain, whose facade will be viewed until we pass Lower Pine Lake. From the pass the trail drops steeply by rocky switchbacks to Granite Park. This large, rocky cirque is puddled with the lake remnants of a glacial stage which is a constant reminder to the trail traveler of the forces that shaped this terrain. The trail then descends steadily, encountering sparse lodgepole pine just before arriving at a meadow on the inlet stream of Honeymoon Lake, several hundred feet above the lake. There is a good campsite here. The bedrock

"Would it embarrass you very much if I were to tell you . . . that I love you?"   Joan Baez, *Daybreak*

over which the inlet stream flows confuses the trail temporarily, and the traveler should keep to the south edge of the lake. Once over this portion, the trail is clear as it undulates gently to join the Pine Creek Pass trail 1 mile beyond.

Turning left (east), our route descends moderately through increasingly dense lodgepole pine, and fords the inlet stream to Upper Pine Lake. The trail then skirts the left side of this lake, looking down on a meadow that is filling the lake from the lower end, and continues the moderate descent through a marshy section just above Pine Lake (seepage from Birchim Lake). Our route skirts the north side of Pine Lake, crosses the outlet stream by a rock dam and log bridge, and begins the steep, open descent to the end of an old mining road. (The abandoned Brownstone mine is marked by corrugated buildings and a tramway.) This descent, steep in some parts, crosses talus and scree that is broken occasionally by juniper, limber pine, whitebark pine and the ubiquitous lodgepole pine. Once on the road, the remainder of the descent is accomplished by a long series of tedious switchbacks. Two dashing streams with yellow-flower-lined banks break the monotony of the descent, and rest breaks taken nearby offer views of the still-active Union Carbide tungsten mine across the canyon, and Owens Valley far down to the east. Leaving this road, the trail re-enters a dense mixed forest cover of Jeffrey, red fir, black cottonwood and quaking aspen, among which grow wild rose, sulfur flower, columbine, tiger lily, currant, Queen Anne's lace and Bridges' pentstemon. The trail is wet as it fords several branchlets of an unnamed creek feeding Pine Creek, and finally it emerges at the pack station at Pine Creek Roadend (7580′).

> "Blessed are they who have nothing to say, and who cannot be persuaded to say it."   Lowell

Access Lateral #4 (McGee Creek Roadend to Tully Hole): The trailhead (8300′) is located at the end of a dirt road, about 2 miles beyond the McGee Creek Pack Station. This 14-mile access lateral is not all on the *Mt. Abbot* quad, and the hiker using this access route should acquire the *Mt. Morrison* quad.

From the parking area at the end of the road, the trail ascends a short distance to a Forest Service gate, where a sign proclaims the eastern boundary of the John Muir Wilderness Area. The route through McGee Creek canyon traverses the north and then the west slope as the trail ascends southerly. The canyon, for the most part, is sage and rabbit-brush covered, but close to the creek, cooling shade may be found under thriving black cottonwood, water birch, rare copper birch, and quaking aspen. Dense willow thickets line the very lip of the creek and make fishing very difficult but rewarding. Like all the eastern-escarpment creeks, McGee Creek is a tumbling, riotous, cold-water stream and as the traveler winds steadily upward through the canyon, the green-lined streambed snakes a parallel course below. Views from the trail are excellent back over Owens Valley, competing for attention with the awe-inspiring skyline to the west.

The trail fords the tiny watercourse emanating from the springs above Horsetail Falls, and jogs back and forth over McGee Creek below the beaver dam. Early-

---

HAIKU

"Pretty butterflies
Be careful of
Pine-needle points
In this gusty wind."   Shusen

---

season high water makes these fords somewhat hazardous. A short distance beyond the beaver dam, the trail crosses McGee Creek via a large felled log, and then ascends more steeply through a narrowing canyon. Occasional juniper begins to appear, mixed with lodgepole, whitebark and limber pine. The trail traverses the eastern side of a long lagoon section of McGee Creek, and then refords the stream. As the trail loops westerly, it becomes steeper and enters a moderately dense lodgepole forest. Via alternately rocky and dusty, duff sections, the trail reaches the Steelhead Lake lateral, where our trail continues, climbing steeply westward over a forested, rocky slope. This ascent borders wildflower-lined McGee Creek, and passes by several "packer" campsites. The trail swings away from the creek, winds through a pleasant lodgepole and mountain-hemlock forest cover, and circles a small tarn before ascending steeply to the rocky, open slopes just below Big McGee Lake (10,480'). If time and inclination allow, one will want to explore the good fishing at nearby Little McGee Lake, Crocker Lake, or picture-book Golden Lake. Those who wish to try their luck for the famous Sierra golden trout can take the faint trail branching left (south) around Big McGee Lake to Upper Hopkins Lakes via Hopkins Pass (southwest from Big McGee Lake). This is a side trip that should be taken only if one has a day to lay over on Hopkins Lakes.

With the colorful, majestic heights of Red and White Mountain looming on the left (southwest), the route ascends by a rocky, winding trail to Little McGee Lake. From Little McGee Lake, our route ascends more sharply through a rocky side canyon to the shaley heights of McGee Pass (11,900').

From the rarefied heights of this lofty saddle, views are excellent of Red Slate Mountain to the north, Red and White Mountain to the south, and the broad, sweeping, high-country meadows around the headwaters of Fish Creek, at the foot of the slope to the west. The vivid reds of the surrounding heights are the product of iron staining of granite and slate, and the buffs and tans are ancient rocks introduced by buckling and folding of the landscape. From the pass, our route descends to Fish

Creek via a series of switchbacks built by the Sierra Club in conjunction with the Forest Service.

The upper drainage basin of Fish Creek is a long, open, grassy meadow of the type some people call "sky-parlor meadows." The trail follows the meandering course of the creek through these grasslands, allowing the traveler who admires wild back-country scenery to absorb the primitive beauty of this area. Anglers, particularly fly fishermen, will find the leisurely pace along Fish Creek satisfying. The trail follows the south bank of Fish Creek (the topo map shows it on the north bank) as it descends below treeline. After crossing Fish Creek, the trail offers fine views of the Silver Divide to the south before descending abruptly to the meadows of

---

"There is but one truly serious philosophical problem, and that is suicide."   Camus

---

Horse Heaven. This descent parallels cascading Fish Creek, and the trail is dusty. The open grasslands of the meadows abound in wildflowers, particularly in early season. From Horse Heaven to Tully Hole the trail is a gradual descent along the north bank of Fish Creek. Like the meadows at Horse Heaven, the grasslands of Tully Hole (9500′) are rife with wildflower color. The stream is sometimes bowered with willows, but the long, swirling, curved line of Fish Creek is for the most part an open, pleasant stretch of water with grassy, overhung banks and several deep holes. The route at this point joins the John Muir Trail.

Lateral #5 (Fish Creek to Mono Creek): This 8-mile cross-country lateral should be undertaken by experienced backpackers only, as the Silver Divide crossing requires some mountaineering skills (rope should be carried and used). This description begins at the point where the outlet stream from Tully Lake joins Fish Creek. Here a fisherman's trail ascends along the south side of the outlet stream (unmarked on the topo map). At the lake our route crosses the outlet stream and ascends the grassy swale that lies due east of the lake. At the outlet stream from Red and White Lake our route turns right (southeast) and follows this stream to the lake itself. Red and White Lake offers an excellent vantage point from which to take in the spectacular and

---

"i thank You God for most this amazing day: for the leaping greenly spirit of trees and a blue true dream of sky; and for everything which is natural which is infinite which is yes"   e. e. cummings

---

aptly named heights of Red and White Mountain. The saddle that this route crosses is clearly discernible on the lowest point of the right shoulder of Red and White Mountain, and the easiest route to the saddle takes the traveler around the rocky east shore of the lake. The steepest part of the ascent is over treacherous shale, and the climber is well-advised to take it slow and easy. From the 11,600′ top of this saddle, we obtain a well-deserved and exciting view of the surrounding terrain. To the north the immediate, dazzling blue of Red and White Lake sets off the buff browns and ochre reds of the surrounding rock. Beyond this basin the meadowy cirque forming the headwaters of Fish Creek is a large greensward that contrasts sharply with the austere, red-stained eminence of Red Slate Mountain, and the distant skyline offers sawtooth profiles of the Ritter Range, with its readily identifiable Minarets, and views of the Mammoth Crest. To the south, the barren, rocky shores of the Grinnell chain of lakes occupy the foreground, and, just beyond, the green-sheathed slopes of the Mono Creek watershed drop away, rising in the distance to the Mono Divide.

Like the ascent to this saddle, the descent should be taken with some care. The sudden, shaley drop terminates in a large "rock garden," a jumble of large boulders just above Little Grinnell Lake. Our rock-hopping route takes us along the east shore of this tiny lake to the long, grassy descent leading to the western side of Grinnell Lake (10,800′). Midway along this side, where the most prominent peninsula infringes on the long lake, our route strikes the marked fisherman's trail that veers southwest down a long swale to tiny Laurel Lake. There are several fair campsites at this junction which offer excellent views due to their situation on a plateau above the lake. Alternative good campsites can be found along the meadowy fringes of Laurel Lake (10,300'), about 1 mile southwest.

The fisherman's trail from Grinnell Lake to Laurel Lake descends via a long, scooplike swale to the grassy meadows forming the headwaters of Laurel Creek. The trail, though very faint from Grinnell to Laurel Lake, becomes clearer as it descends gently along Laurel Creek. At this point the creek is still a "jump-across" stream. The gradual descent along the creek becomes somewhat steeper just above the larger meadows. The pleasant, timber-fringed grassland is divided by the serpentine curves of Laurel Creek. The trail across the meadow is difficult to follow, and the traveler who loses it should cross to the west side of Laurel Creek and look for the trail in the vicinity of the campsites at the south end of the meadow. The dense lodgepole cover at the end of the meadow soon gives way to chaparral thickets and occasional clumps of quaking aspen as the trail reaches the steep, switchbacking descent above Mono Creek. These switchbacks are unmaintained, and are subject to heavy erosion. However, the difficult going is more than compensated for by the excellent views across the Mono Creek watershed into the Second Recess. Particularly impressive are the heights of Mt. Gabb and Mt. Hilgard, which guard the upper end of this feeder canyon. The final descent to the Mono Creek/Mono Pass main trail is a steep, dusty drop.

Access Lateral #6 (Vermilion Campgrd. to John Muir

Trail via Goodale Pass): This 10-mile western access lateral is an interesting way to cross the Silver Divide, and it makes a fine first leg of trips exploring the Fish Creek basin. The description begins at Vermilion Campground (1 mile west of *Mt. Abbot* quad's western boundary) at the west end of Lake Thomas A. Edison, and proceeds along the northern edge of the lake via a well-maintained trail (not shown on the topo map). The first, heavily timbered mile from the trailhead is partly on a Forest Service access road and partly on sandy trail. Beginning in dense stands of Jeffrey pine, the road and then the trail wind eastward. This artificial lake, created by the Southern California Edison Company, fills Vermilion Valley.

Our trail passes the trail that forks left (north) to Devil's Bathtub, crosses the bridge over Cold Creek, and then branches left (north) at the Goodale Pass trail junction. This ascent is at first gradual, but soon it becomes steeper. As the elevation increases, the forest cover consists more of lodgepole pine and red fir, and as the trail veers easterly at the crest of the climb, there are several fine vantage points looking into the country to the south and east. Among the landmarks visible from these points are Mono Divide, Recess Peak, Mt.

Campfires are Potential Forest Fires!
"Man is born unto trouble, as the sparks fly up-ward."   *Job 5:7*

Abbot, Mt. Dade and Mt. Mills. From the crown of the climb it is a short ½ mile to the point where the trail rejoins Cold Creek at the foot of Graveyard Meadows (8800′).

From the south end of Graveyard Meadows, the trail winds the length of this subalpine meadow along the east side of meandering Cold Creek. At the end of the meadow, the trail fords the tiny outlet stream from Arrowhead Lake, and re-enters a forest cover of lodgepole and red fir. This forested duff trail ascends the narrowing Cold Creek valley, fording the creek in two places to emerge at the south end of Upper Graveyard Meadow. Smaller than Graveyard Meadows, this rolling grassland shows a forest fringe more alpine in character: mountain hemlock, lodgepole pine, and occasional silver and Jeffrey pine.

In the middle of Upper Graveyard Meadow the Graveyard Lakes trail branches left (good camping and fishing at the lakes), while our route turns right and soon fords Cold Creek. The trail then stepladders up through a series of charming, green pocket meadows, and as it begins switchbacking there are fine views of the cirque at the head of Cold Creek. As the trail nears Goodale Pass the ascent becomes steep, and the trail surface rocky. From Goodale Pass (11,000′ on the topo map, though the sign at the pass reads 11,467′) the panorama includes the Ritter Range to the north and Mono Divide to the south. The descent on the north side of the pass is through barren alpine country with occasional clumps of stunted lodgepole pine and heather. The rocks show the usual signs of glaciation—polish, rounding and striation—and they serve as hiding places for several families of marmots. This descent levels briefly as it crosses the meadowed outlet of Warrior Lake, and then descends gently to join the John Muir Trail.

Lateral #7 (Rosemarie Meadow to Marie Lake): Beginning at Rosemarie Meadow (on the John Muir Trail), this 16.5-mile cross-country lateral makes an alpine circuit of Gemini and The Pinnacles. At the signed junction in Rosemarie Meadow, our route leaves the John Muir Trail, westward over an easy ridge to Lou Beverly Lake. (This well-established trail is not shown on the topo map.) The moderate forest cover of lodgepole through which the trail winds shows the effects of the higher altitude. The 2-needled trees take on a stunted appearance and one begins to see occasional hemlock and clumps of mountain heather. The signed trail to Sandpiper Lake crosses the marshy inlet to Lou Beverly Lake, and ascends along the north and east side of the stream connecting the two lakes. This ascent, over

---

The Fly

"God in His wisdom made the fly
And then forgot to tell us why."

Ogden Nash

rough, unmaintained trail, is steady until it reaches the abrupt granite face just below Sandpiper Lake, where the going becomes very steep. The waterfall outlet of Sandpiper Lake (10,480') makes a musical accompaniment to end the climb by. This lake is an excellent base camp for fishing and hiking excursions to the surrounding lakes on the headwaters of Bear Creek.

Our rugged cross-country loop begins by rounding the south end of Sandpiper Lake and fording the inlet stream coming from Medley Lakes. From here the route ascends southeast by means of the granite ledge systems. Following the south fork of the east inlet stream to Medley Lakes, this route ascends steeply over smoothed, barren granite slabs and grassy pockets to a narrow unnamed lake at the head of the stream on the topo map. From the unnamed lake, we ascend the drainage to the northeast, to an obvious saddle. Just short of this saddle, one has superlative views to the west, and these views are matched to the east when the crest of the saddle is reached. Route-finding on these rugged talus slopes is difficult at best, but the hiker can find a traverse around the steep north slope of Gemini, first descending somewhat and then ascending back to 12,000' just before descending past the unnamed scree-ridden lake just north of Aweetasal Lake.

The rock cairn at the saddle marks a point from which one can see the Sierra crest as it dwindles away to the southernmost skyline. Immediately on the right are the twin peaks of Gemini and the spectacular jumbled crest of The Pinnacles. It is the latter that dominate the views to the west for the remainder of our progress down the East Pinnacles Creek drainage. Descent into this drainage is first moderate (to the first unnamed, talus-cluttered lake), and then steeper as one drops down to shallow Aweetasal Lake. Typical of most of the lakes on this drainage, Aweetasal has virtually no timber, and is broken by tundralike grassy spots between granite slabs.

This is perennial ice-touched land, always cold, and yet a place where one can come by a severe sunburn. Harsh and uninviting as the land seems, the hiker soon finds a beauty to wonder at as he progresses down the drainage. Only those who dare this harshness manage to view The Pinnacles from the east side, and that rugged, spiring rock mass towers on the right as one scrambles down the alternately moderate and steep granite slabs between Aweetasal and Jawbone lakes. Following the outlet stream from Jawbone Lake, one arrives at shallow, grassy Council Lake. Here route-finding becomes simpler as the going levels off, and by a series of grassy benches one passes Paoha and Negit lakes, and, rounding a granite shoulder, comes to Big Moccasin Lake. Stunted and solitary whitebark pines, a sure sign of high alpine country, dot the rocky fringes of this shallow lake. From Big Moccasin Lake it is an easy descent to Little Moccasin Lake, where one has fine views of the Piute Creek drainage.

Our route veers due west, descending a grassy chute to the outlet streams from the upper lakes. From the west fork of East Pinnacles Creek this cross-country route swings around the south end of The Pinnacles on a long talus and boulder traverse to the area just north of Pemmican Lake. After the drainage of West Pinnacles Creek is reached, a slight descent past several tarns unmarked on the topo map leads to Spearpoint Lake, which, unlike the lakes of the East Pinnacles Creek drainage, is deep. The rugged terrain around the edges of Spearpoint Lake determines the best feasible route as one that goes over the easy granite ridge separating Spearpoint and Pendant lakes, and thence north across the marshy section separating Pendant and Big Chief lakes. Skirting the east side of shallow Big Chief Lake, this route ascends on a moderate grade from the meadowed north end of the lake to Old Squaw Lake. Glacially smoothed granite slabs line the lake's edge on all sides, and progress is fairly easy along the east shore. Following the inlet stream, the route ascends steadily to Wampum Lake, and one has reached the cirque-basined headwaters of West Pinnacles Creek.

This bowl-like cirque presents route-picking problems, and some care should be exercised in crossing the sometimes steep west wall, which divides the West Pinnacles Creek drainage from the South Fork of Bear Creek drainage. At the top of this wall one has a panoramic vista of Seven Gables, Gemini, The Pinnacles, Emerald Peak, Mt. Henry, Mt. Senger, Mt. Hooper and the Bear Creek drainage. Descent from this ridge presents no problems to the accomplished rock-climber, but the easiest route for the novice is found by picking one's way westward around the head of the Three Island Lake cirque to the saddle just east of Sharp Note Lake, and then traversing down the steep slopes on the west side of Three Island Lake. Keeping to the west side of the lake, this route then ascends the easy, tarn-dotted swale at the southwest end of Sandpiper Lake. This line of route takes one around the granite-slabbed nose of the ridge extending north from Mt. Senger. From the nose of the ridge, one has excellent views down the Bear Creek drainage. Turning toward the south, we look into the immense cirque basin headed by Mt. Senger. From the top of this ridge, it is a moderate descent to large, granitoid Marie Lake, where our route skirts the meadowy northern edge. Walking the turfy fringes of the lake one will find lousewort and western mountain aster mixed among the heather. This lake fringe marks timberline, and as our route turns south on the west side of Marie Lake, the mixed sparse forest of hemlock and lodgepole pine is left behind. At the outlet of Marie Lake our route rejoins the John Muir Trail as it winds along the west banks of the lake.

Travel

THERE ARE THREE METHODS used to travel the trails described in this book. They are 1) on foot, either by daywalks or with a backpack; 2) on horseback, with or without a pack string; or 3) on foot while leading a burro or a mule. Motorized vehicles are outlawed in Wilderness Areas and on trails in National Parks. The method one decides upon should take into account the purpose of the trip (fishing, nature study, photography, cross-country walking, etc.), grazing restrictions, personal condition (health, age), and length of time one plans to spend in the back country.

The most popular of the three is to go on foot with a backpack. The reasons given for this choice by backpackers are that they feel backpacking lets one get "closer to the country," and that backpacking is more economical. Travel on horseback is a second choice employed by those who like the principle of long-term base camps, and/or those who are physically incapable of traveling long distances on foot. Those who lead burros or "walking mules" are, by definition, in-betweeners. (Note: Availability of burros and "walking mules" should be determined with packers before deciding upon this method.)

Backpackers

SIERRA BACKPACK-ers are serious individu-alists, and they are never more serious than when they are talking about their equipment. Because they carry their gear on their backs, they tend to make lightweight equipment a fetish—to the point of sometimes forgetting their purpose for taking to the back country. Accordingly, the following list stresses the basics without a lengthy discussion of comparative differences of style.

BACKPACK EQUIPMENT

Necessary

pack
bedroll
extra socks
cooking pot(s)
spoon
maps
compass
flashlight
first aid kit
ground sheet
plastic tarp

line
toilet paper
waterproof matches
warm jacket
knife
soap
raingear
bandana
plastic bags
boots
Sierra cup

Optional

foam pad/air mattress
stove
fuel container
canteen
tent
hat
insect repellent
toothbrush and paste

hiking shorts
paper towels
fork
prescriptions
extra clothing
notebook and pencil
ice axe
crampons

lip salve
sun-tan lotion
dark glasses
climbing rope

salt/pepper shaker
bowl
cooking pots
gloves

Luxury

mirror
wire grill
fishing gear
fishing license
air pillow
camp shoes
wrist watch
camera
binoculars

pot grippers
harmonica
recorder
guitar
sewing kit
wash basin
books
small towel

Packers

THOSE WHO PROVIDE RENTal stock and guides for back-country trips into the Sierra are called "packers." Packers do not make a practice of outfitting their customers beyond the requisite stock, saddles and gearbags. Their usual service includes guiding, and the customer has the alternative of having the stock and the wrangler/guide along for the duration of the trip, or asking for a "spot trip." The latter is an agreement between packer and guests that they and their gear will be transported to a designated campsite, and that the packer will return at a stipulated time to transport them back to the trailhead.

Reservation arrangements for a packer's services should be made well in advance, and should include the following information in the initial correspondence:

1. How many persons will there be in your party?

2. Approximately what dates will you want to pack in and pack out?

3. To what lakes or to what area do you wish to pack?

4. If you have a route preference (perhaps described in this book) what is it?

5. Will you want the continuous hire of the packers and animals, or will you want a spot trip?

6. How many pounds do you estimate your pack load will be?

Prices for packers' services vary, and should be determined by correspondence with the individual packer.

Whether on horseback or afoot, the basic clothing to be worn on the trail is the same. One should wear a long-sleeved shirt, durable trousers, light-weight inner socks (usually cotton), heavy outer socks (usually wool), and boots (riding boots/vibram-soled hiking boots). The following should be carried on one's person: knife, map, compass, matches, rubber bands, pencil, bandana, identification, Sierra cup.

"A mule has neither pride of ancestry nor hope of posterity."   Robert Ingersoll

WEST SIDE

D AND F PACK STATION	Floyd Fike, Box 118, Lakeshore, Calif. 93634
HIGH SIERRA PACK STATION	Tom Cunningham, Mono Hot Springs, Calif. 93642
LOST VALLEY CAMP	Fred Ross, Lakeshore, Calif. 93634

EAST SIDE

MAMMOTH PACK OUTFIT	Lou Roeser, Mammoth Lakes, Calif. 93546
McGEE CREEK PACK STATION	Box 1044 Bishop, Calif. 93514
RED'S MEADOW PACK TRAIN	Arch Mahan, Mammoth Lakes Post Office, Box 395, 93546
PINE CREEK SADDLE AND PACK TRAIN	Slim Nivens or R. Douglas Bottorf, Pine Creek Pack Station, Bishop, Calif. 93514
ROCK CREEK PACK STATION	Herbert London, Box 248, Bishop, Calif. 93514
SCHOBER PACK TRAIN	Art Schober, Box 458, Bishop, Calif. 93514

Climbers

EVEN AS BACKPACKERS are considered serious individualists, climbers have a reputation of snobbery. Far from the stereotyped daredevil, the usual climber is addicted to methodical disciplines, and not all of his climbs are made over thousands of feet of exposure while hanging by his fingernails. Climbs are rated by their difficulty beginning with class I and going through class VI (now Class A, standing for Aided). The following list is compiled of the peaks within the quadrangle of the class I and II variety. These climbs can be made without rope, and with a minimum of scrambling. (Many of these peaks are without names; they are identified by their elevations as shown on the topographic map. Some of these peaks also have more difficult routes, as well as Class I or II routes; see *Mountaineer's Guide to the High Sierra*.)

Named Peaks

Gemini	Mt. Gabb	Mt. Stanford
Graveyard Peak	Mt. Hooper	Mt. Starr
Merriam Peak	Mt. Hopkins	Pilot Knob
Mono Rock	Mt. Huntington	Red & White Mtn.
Mt. Crocker	Mt. Julius Caesar	Royce Peak
Mt. Dade	Mt. Senger	Seven Gables

Unnamed Peaks

11,336	12,067	12,252
11,363	12,178	12,408
11,669	12,205	12,522
11,919	12,221	12,831
12,014	12,238	12,866

Bibliography

BOOKS

American Red Cross, *First Aid Textbook,* Corrected and Revised; Philadelphia.

*Farquhar, Francis P., *History of the Sierra Nevada,* University of California Press, Berkeley, 1965.

*Farquhar, Francis P., *Place Names of the Sierra Nevada,* Sierra Club, San Francisco, 1926 (out of print).

Fletcher, Colin, *The Complete Walker,* Alfred A. Knopf, New York, 1969.

*Gudde, Edwin G., *California Place Names: A Geographical Dictionary,* University of California Press, Berkeley, 1949.

*Hinds, Norman E. A., *Evolution of the California Landscape,* Division of Mines Bulletin #158, San Francisco, 1952.

*Hoover, M. B., *et al.,* *Historic Spots in California,* Stanford, California, 1966.

*Jepson, Willis L., *Manual of the Flowering Plants of California,* University of California Press, Berkeley, 1923.

Manning, Harvey, ed., *Mountaineering, the Freedom*

*Indicates specific information about the country mapped in the *Mt. Abbot* quadrangle can be found in this book or pamphlet.

of the Hills, The Mountaineers, Seattle, 1960.

*Muir, John, *My First Summer in the Sierra,* Houghton Mifflin Company, Boston, 1911.

*Munz, Philip A., *California Mountain Wildflowers,* University of California Press, Berkeley, 1963.

Murie, Olaus J., *Field Guide to Animal Tracks,* Houghton Mifflin, Boston, 1958.

Parsons, Mary Elizabeth, *The Wild Flowers of California,* Dover Publications, New York, 1966.

Peattie, Roderick, ed., *The Sierra Nevada: The Range of Light,* Vanguard Press, New York, 1947.

Peterson, Roger Tory, *Field Guide to Western Birds,* Houghton Mifflin, Boston, 1968.

*Roth, Hal, *Pathway in the Sky (The Story of the John Muir Trail),* Howell-North, Berkeley, 1965.

*Sierra Club, *Mountaineer's Guide to the High Sierra,* Sierra Club, San Francisco, 1972.

Sierra Club, *Going Light with Backpack or Burro (How to Get Along on Wilderness Trails),* Sierra Club, San Francisco, 1964.

*Starr, Walter A., Jr., *Guide to the John Muir Trail and the High Sierra Region,* Sierra Club, San Francisco, 1968.

Storer, T. I., and Usinger, R. L., *Sierra Nevada Natural History (An Illustrated Handbook),* University of California Press, Berkeley, 1963.

Sudworth, George B., *Forest Trees of the Pacific Slope,* Dover Publications, New York, 1967.

PAMPHLETS

*Dresser, Lettie G., *A 1916 Honeymoon in the Sierra*, Dresser, Fresno, California, 1964.

*Elsasser, A. B., *Indians of Sequoia and Kings Canyon National Parks*, Sequoia Natural History Association, Three Rivers, California.

*Matthes, Francois E., *Reconnaissance of the Geormorphology and Glacial Geology of the San Joaquin Basin, Sierra Nevada, California* (Professional Paper 329), U. S. Government Printing Office.

Thomas, Winnie and Bunnelle, Hasse, *Food for Knapsackers*, Sierra Club, San Francisco, 1964.

OTHER WILDERNESS PRESS PUBLICATIONS

*Denison, Don, and Winnett, Thomas, *Sierra Nevada Place Names Guide*, Wilderness Press, Berkeley, 1969.

*Schwenke, Karl, and Winnett, Thomas, *Sierra North*, 100 Back-Country Trips in California's Sierra, Wilderness Press, Berkeley, 1967.

*Schwenke, Karl, and Winnett, Thomas, *Sierra South*, 100 Back-Country Trips in California's Sierra, Wilderness Press, Berkeley, 1968.

*——— *High Sierra Fishing Guide to Mono Creek*, Wilderness Press, Berkeley, California, 1968.

*——— *High Sierra Fishing Guide to French Canyon-Humphreys Basin*, Wilderness Press, Berkeley, California, 1968.

Trail Profiles

The trail profiles on the following pages will help the hiker in his planning. With a pack of about 1/5 your body weight, you can expect to cover two horizontal miles per hour. Add one hour for each 1000 feet of elevation gain. Thus, if you are going 12 miles, and the total of all the "ups" is 1500 feet, you can expect to be walking for about: 6 hours + 1.5 hours = 7½ hours. This includes "normal" rest stops.

For downhill walking, use the figure of two miles per hour except where the trail is steep. A steep section will require an extra hour for 2000 feet of descent.

If you are walking without a pack, or you are in really excellent condition, you can do better — perhaps up to 50% better.

If you are walking cross country, it may take you all day to go even two miles. There is wide variation, depending on the slope, the footing, the ground cover, and your condition.

Each numbered trail in the descriptions is represented in the following pages in 5-mile segments, on a scale with a vertical exaggeration of about 250%.

The symbol ⌇ means "ford," but there may be no running water there in the late summer. Since bridges require no fording, they are not shown.

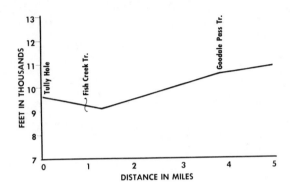

Main trail #1

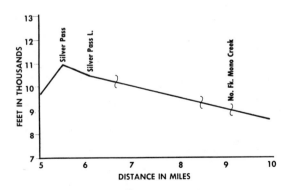

Main Trail #1 continued

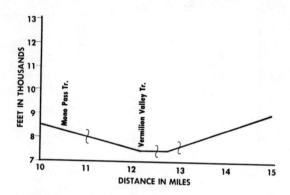

Main Trail #1 continued

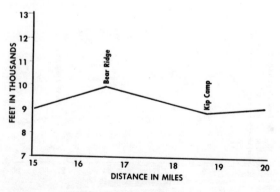

Main Trail #1 continued

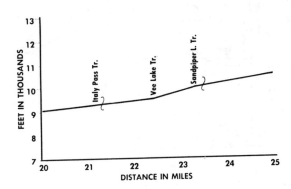

Main Trail #1 continued

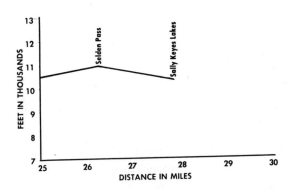

Main Trail #1 continued

74

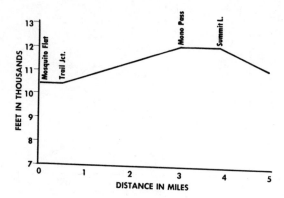

Main trail #2

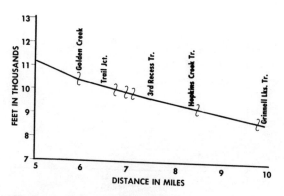

Main trail #2 continued

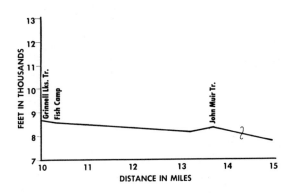

Main trail #2 continued

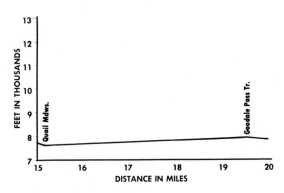

Main trail #2 continued

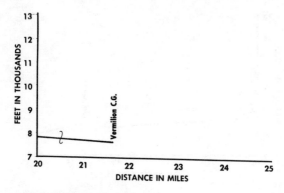

Main trail #2 continued

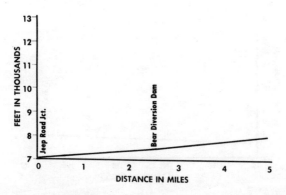

Main trail #3

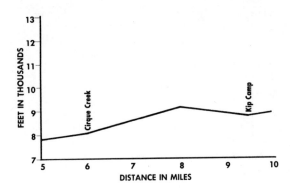

Main trail #3 continued

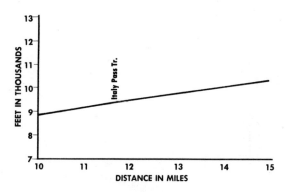

Main trail #3 continued

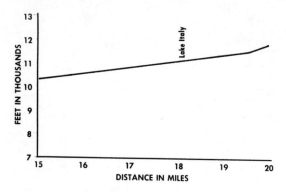

Main trail #3 continued

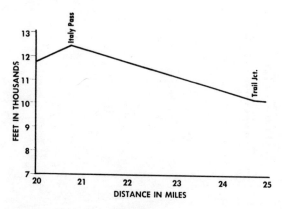

Main trail #3 continued

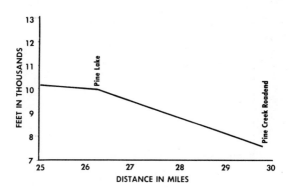

Main trail #3 continued

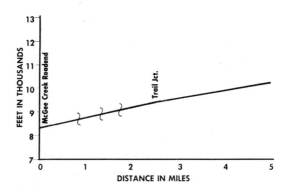

Access lateral #4

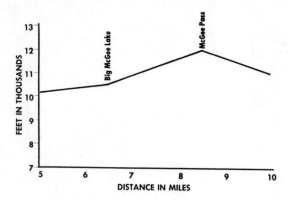

Access lateral #4 continued

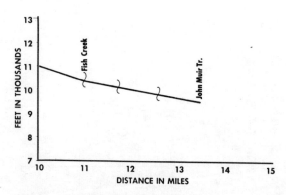

Access lateral #4 continued

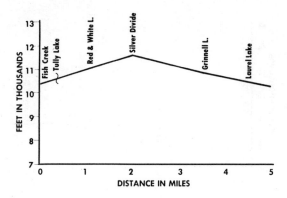

Lateral #5

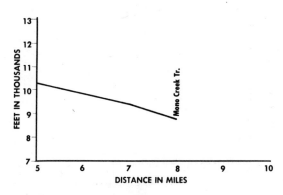

Lateral #5 continued

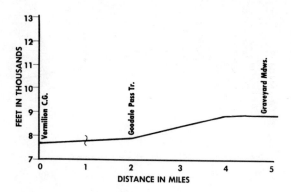

Access lateral #6

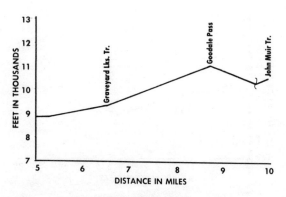

Access lateral #6 continued

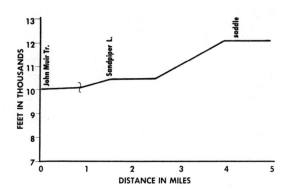

Lateral #7

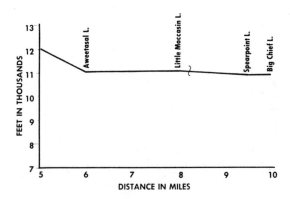

Lateral #7 Continued

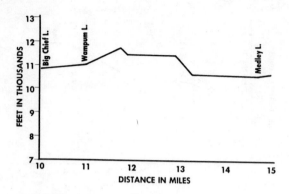

Lateral #7 Continued

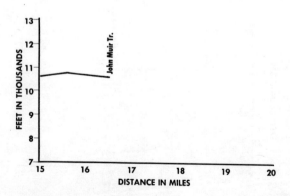

Lateral #7 Continued

Index